For Permission contact:

David Schilling
DavidjSchilling@gmail.com

Edited by: Andrew Fantasia

Dedicated to:
Rachelle, who saved my life more times than I
can count. I love you my Guardian Angel.

Prologue

I wasn't always a hollow shell of a man. In high school I played football, was on the gymnastics team and won drama awards. Sure, I was bullied, but who wasn't? I was just like most other kids; I had a breaking point. The bulling stopped when I started to stand up for myself. Most of the time I could talk my way out of bad situations, but not all the time.

I started coaching gymnastics at 14 and was working almost full time. I was the 'Super Coach'. When people found out about me coaching a 'girl's sport', and watching me in drama class, the names started again. The names didn't bother me at all. I was acting. I loved being able to take on the persona of a different person. I got to do and say all the things I wanted to in character that I couldn't in real life. The name calling stopped when I got into college for acting. I was no longer the "fag actor", we were all actors.

School was intense, but I loved every second of it. I met a bunch of lifelong friends and started my career in acting.

I bought my first camera to take photos of my gymnastics athletes and my love for

Photography was born. As soon as people found out I had a camera, I was asked to take photos for friends. I branched out and started to take fashion photos and boudoir photos and I was even published in a magazine. Photography is a huge passion and I pursue it to this day. It's probably one of my favourite things.

Excluding school, I lived at home until I was 24, when a rough family dynamic caused me to move in with a friend of mine. I didn't want to move out, but it was either that for go insane, so I moved. Things were perfect for the first few months, and even though he was constantly late with rent and his girlfriend made porn in their room, I was free. After being owed a few thousand dollars and never getting all of it back, it was time to move again.

For the first three years on my own, I was a dog trainer. It's the best job ever. I got to spend the day teaching dogs basic commands and manners and I spent the rest of the day playing and petting dogs. I would go in on my days off because my job was stress free. I got to spend 7 days a week playing with dogs. It was perfect. That is until the place closed. I spent almost eight months on unemployment. The worst part about being on unemployment is having to take care of your roommates… again.

I bounced from job to job working for worse and worse bosses and decided to go back to my gymnastics roots. I've missed coaching. I finally made almost enough to pay for my roommates. I took my one day off to host weddings. I got paid to party. *This is great, who needs sleep?*

Apparently, I do. I can't take my boss's abusive behaviour anymore. I want to call the people who are supposed to watch over the gyms, but she sits on the board, and can control everything. I want to call protective services, but she'll lie her way out of that too. I'm having a really hard time working weddings as well. My wedding clients are really getting on my nerves and it's harder to care for my roommates.

In desperation, I finally leave gymnastics behind and go back to dogs, but I just can't keep up. My boss wants me to take a 90 minute drive and make in in less than an hour. He wants me to sign a contract where I make less than minimum wage, and he wants all my ideas. I'm falling apart and I can't take the pressure. My boss wants me to do more and more for less and less and he doesn't care about any of his employees. I can't get out of bed. I hate my life, and my job, and my roommates. Nothing makes me happy. Not even dogs. I'm doing nothing with my life. I'm sinking deeper and deeper and the people I have cared for, for so long, have disappeared.

I have nothing. *I am nothing.*

This is where the story begins, and almost ends.

Almost.

Chapter 1: The fall

I quit! Not at life, not yet. I quit my dog walking job. *What am I going to do for work*? I can't work for another boss. People here don't care about anything other than money. I know, I'll drive for Uber.

Honestly, Uber is fun. I meet awesome people, give them relationship advice, and work my own hours. Things are coming up Milhouse. Until I get into an accident that changes me forever. I'm on the highway in the fast lane, and a car comes out behind me and cuts me off. I swerve to avoid the car and I hit the wall. My two left wheels drove up the wall and take to the air. I crash down on the road and swerve across three lanes of traffic to the other shoulder. I'm afraid to drive. I hate my car. *I hate me.*

Stop!

Something's wrong. This isn't me. I'm David. I'm the happy one. The one that never says anything bad. What's going on? Time to call my doctor.

I wait and wait and wait. I call and call. I get no set answer from my doctor's office, and no appointment. I loved my doctor, and now I feel betrayed, like he doesn't care. It's not fair. He listened to my younger sister, but won't listen to me? *You don't deserve help.* My doctor is supposed to be in my corner, and I can't even see him? Finally, my mother walks into the office and refuses to leave until there's an appointment card in her hand. 18 months after I first call my doctor, I tell him what's going on: I can't drive, I don't want to leave my house and get anxiety when I do. I sleep more and more yet feel less and less rested. Worst of all, I don't like anything about me. His response? 'Mild anxiety' and 'there's nothing I can do'. I spent 18 months waiting to hear from him, for him to tell me there's nothing he can do? I've watched enough TV to know there's something out there for mild anxiety and this isn't mild. When I cry in the car, or while grocery shopping, it's not mild. So, I continue with some physical effects I have. He finally stops me and prescribes me something for 'mild anxiety'.

It's not helping. It's making me feel worse. I'm not sleeping more than three hours a day- yes, a day. I don't sleep at night. I hate myself so much it hurts. I don't know how, but I am in physical pain from hate. Hate for myself.

I don't know what to do so I turn to my roommates for help. I can't drive, so I can't work. I need them to pay for their own bills and maybe keep me a little company. Instead of company, I get ignored. Instead of paying their bills, I get court papers saying rent wasn't paid. My roommates are my family, if they don't love me how can anyone? *If no one   loves   me,   why   stick   around*?

Shut   up!   Shut   up!   Shut   up!

Thoughts like that aren't good. You know that. Call your doctor again and don't take no for an answer.

Finally, my doctor admits things are out of his league and refers me to CAMH: The Centre for Addiction and Mental Health. I quickly max out one medication and start another. Things aren't working. How can I be getting worse on meds? I remember what my psychiatrist said 'It'll get worse before it gets better'. He was right. I got worse. My mind is racing all the time with too many negative thoughts to keep track. In the next second, there are no thoughts at all, just complete emptiness. I feel scared all the time, scared that if I fall asleep, I won't wake up. My body hurts all over, like every bone in my body is broken. I am in so much pain I can't lift my head off the couch.

I do everything I can to make the pain stop: I meditate, I burn incense, I have two salt lamps. I don't want to leave my house, but my dog forces me outside for walks and I smoke a lot of weed. Cannabis is the only thing that I have found that slows my mind down. I can think again, so long as I am high. I try not to smoke too much but being sober   just   lets   the   demons   take   over.

I get a bit of a social life when my best friend asks me to star in his web series. I don't care what it is, I just get to be around people and get to act again.

I'm late to filming on the first day because a dog bite on my left hand sends me to the hospital. When I get home, three people are already filming. My best friend, my one roommate, and one of our actresses. She's, wow... She asks me if she could get me a drink. In my own house. Who does that? She's smart, really funny, and silly. Clearly, she can act, but I catch her singing and she has the most beautiful voice I've heard. Beautiful? Doesn't describe her. She gives me butterflies just looking at her. She's got long dark hair and big beautiful eyes. Catching her laugh forces a smile out of me.

There's something really nice about getting feelings for someone as soon as you meet them. It's very liberating. My mind starts to think of happy things. Our firsthand hold, our first kiss. We would look great together and by that, I mean I would love to date her.

After filming I ask my best friend about her and he responds with two words: 'Rachelle's (pronounced Rachel) taken'. Of course, she is. I've been single for eight years, why on earth would that change now?

Filming is getting harder. When we started, I was on better terms with my roommate. He doesn't know, but I resent him so much for making me poor. I can't work because I can't sleep. I'm living off borrowed money and he's not caring.

Getting to see Rachelle twice a month is the only highlight to my life. Hearing her voice focuses my mind. Watching her laugh at her own mistakes brings me happiness. I want to tell her how much my heart wants to explode when our eyes meet, but the swelling in my throat won't let the words out. I want to spend every second of every day with her. I don't spend time with the cast because I can't even look at my roommate.

I'm not eating, not sleeping, not working. I keep increasing my medications and it's not helping. I'm getting worse not better. The only thing keeping me alive is the weed I smoke quieting my mind. I'm a burden to my friends and family. *End the burden.*

Where's the shut up?

Chapter 2: The Bottom

There's a weird silence at rock bottom. There are no voices speaking hate, no demons to fight. There's no need. They've already done their job and now they sit back and watch their handywork. To be honest, I miss the voices. I am alone in life, so they gave me someone to talk to.

I have nothing and no one. I'm not living. I'm existing. If you're not living, why stick around? I take any old rope I have lying around, tie myself an old-fashioned hangman's noose, and hide the rope. Don't need someone seeing this. Now is not the time. I need to finish filming first.

Filming is impossibly hard. I'm trying to be positive but it's fake and empty. No one notices, which is nice. *Apparently, I'm a better actor than I thought*. Being around the other actors makes me tired. I must pretend to like my roommate, pretend to be happy, pretend I want to live. When I am not filming, I am as far away from people as I can be. Just me and my dog; *the only being on earth that loves me*.

I drill a hole in the ceiling beam in the basement big enough for a rope to fit through and test it to make sure they can both hold my body weight. *No need to make a mistake*.

I cry all the time. Just because the voices are gone, doesn't mean the pain is. I hurt all over for no reason. I sleep on my couch and sometimes the floor, when I do sleep. I was never this person. I might have been shy, but I'm a fighter. I call my psychiatrist and max out my second medication and enroll in behavioural therapy.

The drive home from my psychiatrist is very hard. *I give up*. Two meds, therapy, nothing is working. My friends aren't around. My family hates me. I am alone in the world. *There's no point*. There are no tears with my decision. No sadness. In fact, a weight feels lifted off my back. *This is right. It's time to go*.

I say mental goodbyes to the people I think once cared: my family, my friends, my dog.

My dog. My beautiful dog. I picture her lying under my hanging feet and it makes me cry. *Tears are good*. They mean I'm feeling, which means I care. *I have something to care for*. I get home and hug my dog so hard she wants nothing to do with me. She doesn't know it, but she saved my life.

We get to another film day and something is off. Rachelle is quiet. I want to ask if she's okay, but I'll just get a 'yeah'. I brave sitting with the cast the whole time so I can try and overhear the small talk. It sucks. My spying pays off when I overhear Rachelle tell another cast member that she broke up with her boyfriend. She's single! *Just feel bad for her pain, it's not like you're going to say anything.*

After everyone leaves, I send a text to Rachelle offering sympathy for her lost relationship. She thanks me and tells me that it's for the best as he wasn't a great guy. She then calls me the 'F' word. Friend. If ever there was a relationship defining word, it's friend.

My one roommate owes me more than four thousand dollars. It's ridiculous. I'm not working, and I am still paying his bills. My other roommate owes me more than a thousand. I've had enough. I text my roommate telling him he owes me too much money and needs to pay for his own bills as well as pay me back. He responds with 'we'll talk tomorrow'.

My roommate is annoyed that I keep bringing up the money he owes me. He accuses me of being lazy, and selfish, and only caring about myself. My other roommate cripples me. He calls me racist and sexist and accuses me of sexual assault.

WHAT? In all my years of life, I have always erred on the side of caution and it's held me back in my life. How can I have sexually assaulted anyone? The rest of the conversation fades out. My mind goes dark and I start to cry. Once again,

I get called selfish for making things about me. I get up to take my dog for a walk and fall over. I have no feeling in my legs and can't see. I finally get to my feet and take my dog outside. How could they have come out with all of this? I just wanted them to pay their share.

I don't sleep for a minute. I am up all night thinking about all the things that I was called. I feel sick. I throw up outside in my backyard. The next day both roommates come down to the living room with papers in their hands. They both have written down what they owe me and have me sign a payment agreement at twenty dollars a week. I have no option. If I want my money, I have to sign. It's going to take years for them to pay it off, but at least they will pay it off.

They stand in front of me and tell me that they are moving out. It's a week into November, and they are moving out? Things just get worse. I ask them if they've taken care of their rent and they tell me they have. Okay. At least I don't have to worry about rent for November, just for December. I don't think anything of it again until I get another notice telling me rent wasn't paid. They flat out lied to my face and got away with not paying rent for their last month here. At least they're gone. I don't have to see them anymore. I get the house to myself.

Rachelle invites the cast to a seminar and only two of us go. *Of course I go, Rachelle invited me*. It's not really my cup of tea, but I'm out with Rachelle, so I don't care.

I head back home and the happiness I felt fades into nothingness. I've liked Rachelle since the day I met her, but she only sees me as a friend. Story of my life.

Chapter 3: The Change

In an effort to stay sane, I start an internet channel called 'Chilling with Schilling'. My best friend and Rachelle volunteer to be the first guests. Filming is fun and Rachelle is absolutely hilarious. *She's amazing*. We finish shooting and end up talking for another hour. Before they leave, Rachelle offers to pick up some weed as I am running low. I accept her offer. It means I get to see her again. It's late and they leave. Today was incredible.

I'm about to go to bed when I get a message from Rachelle telling me not to worry about paying her for the weed. I don't take well to kindness, so I ask why. She tells me she's had feelings for me since the day she's met me.

Wait, what?

I read her messages over and over again to make sure I'm not dreaming. I read that right; she likes me. My whole body goes numb. I can't think straight. She finishes by telling me not to rush my response, which is all I want to do. *Arms, brain, please work*.

I tell her I feel the same way about her and can't believe the turn our conversation took. We make plans for her to come down to visit the next day. *That's tomorrow.* It can't come soon enough.

On her way to my house, I get a video message from Rachelle. It's a love song on the radio and she says in the video "I'm actually crying". Who is this woman? I've never had anyone like me this much before. I already don't deserve her, and I haven't even seen her yet.

We spend all day lying together talking and watching TV. I ask her if she wants to do anything and she kisses me and says 'that'. She tells me that she wants to take things slow, as she just ended a bad relationship. I don't care how slow we take things, she's mine and that's all that matters. As Rachelle gets ready to leave, I give her a kiss and "I love you" slips out. *I'm an idiot.* It's only been a day. She smiles and says "And I love you". So much for taking things slow.

Rachelle is throwing a party at her condo before she sells it. The only downside to going is that she still doesn't want her family knowing about us, because she's afraid they're going to freak out. It's okay, it just means I have to keep my hands to myself. There are so many people here. Lots of her friends and family are here. I meet as many people as I can and make a point to shake the hands of both of her parents and try to get them to laugh. *I hope they like me.* Rachelle gets everyone's attention and starts to speak. She tells us that she is a big advocate for mental health as she suffers from depression. I want to advocate for mental health too. *She's perfect!* Her friends are amazing. I am laughing without faking. I haven't felt this happy in a long time.

We invite each other everywhere. I go with her to return some things to a store. I help her out of the car, and she takes my hand. It fits perfectly with mine. Every cheesy love song that I can think of blasts through my mind. *I am going to marry this woman.* We go out for walks and coffee, and dancing, and to the movies, but our favourite thing to do is cuddle. We can't get close enough to each other when we do. When we are together, we are joined at the hip. She brings me such peace. We both have depression. We both have good days and bad days, but the bad days are easier because she's beside me.

I have to move back to my parent's house. *This sucks!* Stupid roommates draining me dry. I now live over an hour from Rachelle, but the distance doesn't phase Rachelle at all. She's making me feel like nothing's going to change. My parents come to help me move and I introduce Rachelle as my girlfriend. The first chance my mom gets, she pulls me aside and tells me how much she loves Rachelle already.

Her parents still don't know about us so she tells them her girlfriend lives where I am so she can come visit me regularly without suspicion. Every time I see Rachelle, my eyes light up like I'm seeing her for the first time. She makes me feel so loved. It helps, it helps me so much.

Chapter 4: The Rise

Rachelle is the only good thing going on in my life and things couldn't be better. I feel such peace when I am with her. Rachelle is my home.

The voices are back and so are my demons. They have a new target, but Rachelle's voice is louder. When her voice doesn't help, her hugs do.

I go to a club for her friend's birthday. I hate clubs. I love to dance, but there are too many people, and the music is never good. It's my first time really meeting her friends, so I suck it up and go. I feel anxious and claustrophobic, but I still dance. Rachelle isn't used to my white dance moves, so she laughs and laughs. Her laugh is the greatest sound in the world.

I'm on welfare. I get a whopping $700 a month. Doing anything is next to impossible, but it's better than doing nothing. I spend all my money on weed and seeing Rachelle. She still doesn't want her parents knowing, so she comes to me a lot. Breakfast dates are the best, especially after she stays over. Depression always wakes me up at 3:30 am and Rachelle is always awake with me. She sings until I fall asleep, I can't imagine being with anyone else.

Her patience is unmatched. I miss Easter and she doesn't bat an eyelash. When I missed Valentine's day, she gave me a love letter telling me she'd always be there for me.

I reach out to a friend of mine for legal advice. She tells me a lot of good news regarding my roommates. She also gives great news to Rachelle about her ex boyfriend. I'm going to sue my roommates and finally get what I deserve.

I hate my birthday. I've always been made to feel terrible on my birthday, so I stopped celebrating at 14. It makes me so uncomfortable that I don't tell people when it is and I don't acknowledge it at all. Instead of celebrating, Rachelle comes down the night before and gives me an owl plushie as an I Love You gift. It's perfect. I spray it with her perfume, so my room smells like her when she's not around. We sleep through the whole night. We don't wake up at our usual time. I haven't slept through the night in almost a year. I am going to marry this woman.

I feel horrible, guilty and ashamed. I haven't been able to see Rachelle much lately. She's been busy with work and I am having a hard time paying for gas to see her. Today is the day Rachelle wants to tell her parents about us, so I find some change to pay for gas and drive to her. I am so excited for today. I've been waiting for this moment for months. I make sure to leave my house early, so I don't rush my drive. I always rush when I am excited. *Just keep it slow.*

We sit side by side and she calls her parents into the kitchen. She takes my hand and tells them we are a couple. My heart almost explodes. I'm both scared and excited. We can finally see each other on a regular basis. We don't have to make excuses to see each other. They ask us for how long and we tell them six months. The looks on their faces said it all. After a few 'I knew it's' they were happy for us both. We were free to be us.

We take turns staying at each other's place. I hate staying at her place. I like sleeping in my own bed or on my own couch. Her place doesn't feel like home to me. I know it's not my home, but it's warm and stuffy, and I get bad anxiety staying out of my own place, but I stay over as often as I can. Her mom likes to comment on how we are always joined at the hip. Doesn't matter to us because we are always joined at the hip. Any time we are together, we are holding hands, or she's resting her head on my lap as we are watching tv. My favourite is when she holds me so tightly my arms start to fall asleep.

Today is a big day, we're going to her friend's wedding. She's a bridesmaid and is wearing a light blue strapless dress. It goes down to the floor. Her hair and makeup look absolutely perfect. My Rachelle looks heavenly. All her friends come up to me, telling me how much they've heard about me, and how much they love us as a couple. I can't help but agree. I love us as a couple too. I sit down for dinner and have a wonderful conversation with my table. I meet another photographer and some more friends of Rachelle's. I can't wait for the dancing to start. The head table is pretty far away and that's where Rachelle is. I promise my table a dance for everyone, but once the music starts, I go to the head table, grab Rachelle and start to dance. For the rest of the night, I never leave her side. I feel bad for my table as I completely abandoned them, but it doesn't matter. I have Rachelle.

It's my turn to bring Rachelle to a wedding. My younger sister is getting married, so this will be my chance to introduce her to my extended family. I couldn't much care what they think, as Rachelle is perfect, but it will be nice for them to meet the future Mrs. Schilling. The first chance she gets, my younger sister pulls me aside and tells me how much she loves Rachelle, and how happy I look. *I do look happy.* Slowly throughout the day, my whole family says the same. They all absolutely love Rachelle. I love her. My family loves her. I am in the wedding party, so Rachelle takes control of my camera and takes some wonderful photos of the ceremony for my sister. Watching Rachelle dance with my younger sister and cousins makes me so happy. She fits right in with everyone.

I go to Rachelle's house for a family gathering. We go to a rib festival. I love ribs! I drive so her family can enjoy themselves. I can't drink anyway because of the medication I'm on, so I don't mind at all. We have such a peaceful time sitting in the sun until a young drunk guy runs into Rachelle's mom. We quickly shoo him away and continue to listen to the music. I love spending time with Rachelle's family. They make me feel comfortable. They make me feel home. On the way back to the house, Rachelle's parents sing loudly to the radio. I take Rachelle by the hand and tell her that this is what it's going to be like having kids. She smiles at me and I give her a wink. She squeezes my hand and tells me she loves me. I could hear her say that over and over again.

I make an appointment to see my family doctor to get him to sign disability papers. I am not well enough to work yet. I can barely string two days of leaving the house together. Leaving for hours at a time I can do on a good day, but it takes a few days to recover. I am on welfare, but it isn't providing me with enough money. Without looking at my papers, or asking me any questions, my doctor tells me he's not going to sign my disability papers. *You failed.* He says that he expects me to get back into the work force one day and it's going to take him three hours to sign the papers. I'm frozen. I can't move and I feel my heart stop beating. I feel completely worthless. I feel like a fraud. *Why wouldn't he listen to me*?

For the first time in a long time, thoughts of death fill my mind. I don't know where to turn. My psychologist is on holidays and my parents love my doctor, so they won't care. I call Rachelle and tell her I am not doing so well. I tell her that I am at the end of my rope and without missing a beat, she drives down and the first thing she does is climb into bed with me. She doesn't say anything, she just kisses my forehead and holds me until I fall asleep. I take her to breakfast the next morning and we go for a nice walk through my neighbourhood. She sees an open house and asks me if I want to go pretend, we are looking. I tell her that I am getting tired and want to head back, but I promise the next time she comes down, we will. We spend a few more hours together until I'm in a better place. As she gets into her car, I give her a long kiss and tell her I love her.

I go to Rachelle's house for her dad's birthday. She tells me I don't have to, and if I'm honest, I don't want to go. My anxiety is pretty bad today, but it's important, so I decide to go anyways. Dinner is amazing. Her dad makes kabobs and her mom makes an amazing mango salad. After dinner, we set up a scrabble game. Rachelle and I arc on a team, her mom and dad are on a team, and her younger sister and buyfricnd are on a team. Rachelle cleans house, not once, but twice. The first game she may have been using her phone to look up some words, and in the second she might have used some help on the two letter words, but we still won. It's getting late and my anxiety is through the roof so I get ready to leave. Rachelle is sad. She had a long day at work and was hoping I was staying over, but she understands. I hate seeing Rachelle sad. I wish I could stay, but if I don't go home and relax, I am going to panic. I ask her to come down after she's done work tomorrow and she tells me she will. She kisses me and tells me she loves me. Every kiss I get from Rachelle is a little taste of heaven. I have never been happier in my life.

Chapter 5:

I spend the entire day cleaning. I don't have my phone on me to message Rachelle, but she's coming down anyways and I want to surprise her with a clean room. 8:00 pm comes and she's not here yet. She should be here if she left from work. Maybe she went home to get some things. I grab my phone and check it. No messages. I know she's stressed with work, but she hasn't called or messaged me all day. She would tell me if she was running late. I try to call her and message her a few times, but I don't get an answer. Now I'm worried. What if she was in an accident on the way here? I wait to hear from her but get nothing. I message her mom around midnight and tell myself that if I don't hear from her by morning, I am going to her house.

I wake up to a call at 9:30. It's Rachelle's mom.

"Hello?"
"David…"
"Yes?"
"David…"
"What happened?"
No answer
"I'll be right there!"

I leave my house as fast as I can in my pyjamas and drive faster than I should. My heart hasn't pounded this hard in a long time. I weave in and out of traffic, use the shoulder when I'm not supposed to, and drive like a bat out of hell. On the way, I see a police car pulled over and I ask for help. I start to shake. I tell him something bad happened to my girlfriend. He calls it in on his radio and quickly switches to his phone. He tells me that he's not getting an answer, but I look very visibly distressed. He gives me an escort to Rachelle's house. The whole ride I keep thinking to myself of all the things that could have happened. She was in an accident. What if it wasn't her, but her dad, or her sister? I can help Rachelle through anything, just please let her be okay.

I get to the street before Rachelle's house and my heart leaves me. Time slows down. I look at my speed, and I am doing the limit, but everything feels slower. Here's her street. It's the moment of truth.

Chapter 6: Freefall

I turn onto Rachelle's street and my worst fear comes true. I see two police cars sitting outside of Rachelle's house. One on either side of the street. Neither have their lights flashing. I know instantly that something bad happened to my Rachelle.

"NO!" I scream.

I park as soon as I can and run out of my shoes. I see a beautiful woman with dark hair outside waiting for me. It's Rachelle. She's waiting for me. I run as fast as I can into the arms of Rachelle's sister. She's standing outside their yard waiting for me. As soon as I hug her, my emotions overwhelm me, and I almost fall over. I scream into her shoulder and cry hysterically. The officer who escorted me hugs me and hands me my shoes. Rachelle's sister helps me into the backyard where a group of her family is already. Her uncle hugs me and keeps repeating 'It's just a dream' while tears stream down his face. I'm asked a bunch of questions about Rachelle by the police. I don't know what language they are speaking, or how I am able to answer them. I don't remember how I got here, or what my name is. *You're in shock.* I call my two best friends and tell them the news. They rush over and have the same reaction that I did. The one almost falls over and the other is stunned.

Rachelle's gone. She's actually gone. This isn't happening. I found the girl of my dreams and now she's gone. I sucked the life out of her. It's my fault. The voices are back.

After the police are done talking to me, I walk back to my car. Rachelle's mom asks me where I am going, and I tell her just to the store. I can't be around right now. *I let Rachelle die.* She wanted me to stay over, but I chose to go home. Had I stayed; she'd be alive today.

I get to the corner store and buy my first pack of cigars. I have no weed and I didn't take my meds. My hands are shaking. I need something to keep me together. I'm so out of it that I don't remember getting back to Rachelle's house. I stand in her backyard and light up a cigar. I inhale, hold, and exhale, and don't cough. The cigars keep me from completely letting go, but not much else.

Before the coroner comes to the house, the police let us keep Rachelle company. The rope she used is still attached to the door and it's haunting. *You let her buy that rope.* Rachelle's family is already in her room and crying. I just stare. I have only one emotion: guilt. If her family knew it was my fault, they'd kick me out. *Just say nothing. Murderer.*

After Rachelle leaves her house for the last time, I stay and spend more time with Rachelle's family. I don't know how much time. It's both standing still and moving too fast. *When I get home, I am going to see my Rachelle again.* I think Rachelle's mom read my mind because she sends my two best friends' home with me. I'm officially on suicide watch and I hate everyone for it. *I was the one that should have died, not Rachelle.*

When I get home, my friends sit with me and I just talk. I don't know what I'm saying, or even if it makes sense. I blame myself for her passing. I can't help it. I should have stayed over. *You didn't really love her.* Clearly, I don't sleep at all. My new roommates are awake and checking on me. I can hear them whisper. I think it's them. It could be my mind. I just want to be alone, so I can be with Rachelle again. I pretend to sleep so they don't check in on me as much. I don't want company, I want Rachelle.

The next day I go back to Rachelle's house with a bag of clothes. I pack some things to sleep in so I can stay over for the next week while we get her funeral arrangements in order. Her family is allowing me to be a part of the planning. It works better for me, because I hate my house. I was here when Rachelle passed. I left her for my own bed, and I left her alone. *What's wrong with me*? Why am I more concerned for Rachelle now than I was when she was here? *If I only cared more, she would still be alive*, but her rock wasn't there so she floated away.

I am honoured with being a pallbearer. All I wanted was to take care of Rachelle for the rest of our lives. At least I get to watch over her until the very end. Rachelle's mom insists I read at the service as well. So far everything has been going smoothly, but this is the part I've been dreading-meeting the priest. I have never been a religious person, so I don't have the same connection to the church that her family does and to be honest, I'm afraid. Suicide and the church don't have a good history. We sit down in a meeting room and explain to the priest that Rachelle was an advocate for mental illness and tell him how she passed. He tells us that he is also a mental health advocate and sees the illness Rachelle suffered. He tells us that it's not his place to judge and that Rachelle will get a full catholic funeral. My emotions finally give way. My eyes well up and my heart pounds. For the first time in public, I cry. We explain to him that Rachelle was a beautiful musician and we found a recently unheard song that she wrote. It's a love song she started writing after we met. It's a song about me. We play the song for the priest and I can't sit down. I move to the window and cry. I cry so loud Rachelle's uncle comes and puts his arm around me just before my legs give way. After the song ends, the Priest agrees to let us bring Rachelle into the church to her song. For the first time since her passing, I feel a little peace.

It's time for the first visitation. I'm not keen on being here. I don't know anyone, and I feel so alone. It would be at times like this that Rachelle would grab my hand and introduce me to everyone, whether she knew them or not. I walk through the doors, and head straight to Rachelle. She still looks beautiful in her orange sundress. For the first time in a long time, she looks at peace. She's resting. I kiss her forehead and make my way to a spot in the third row. *First row is for close family, second is for everyone else, and the third row is for you.* Rachelle's sister waves me to the front row of seats. I tell her that I am okay where I am, but I'm dragged to the very front of the line by Rachelle's mom. I had told her mom that I had vows written and wanted to propose. I think she knew I meant it because she started introducing me as Rachelle's fiancé. I haven't felt this connected in a long time. When it's time to open the doors to the public, I am instantly overwhelmed. The line is long, and it doesn't end. I meet hundreds of people. The line is out of the room, into the hallway, through the main entrance, and around a corner to the main parking lot. We go over time by 30 minutes for the first visitation because of how many people loved Rachelle.

Before we take Rachelle to the church, on the day of the funeral, we each take some time alone to say goodbye. I go first. I don't make it all the way to her without falling to my knees and crying. I crawl my way to her casket and just cry on her stomach. I tell Rachelle how much I love her and how much I am going to miss her. *Rachelle, I am so sorry I failed you. You saved me more than once and when you needed me, I went home. You needed me and I waited until morning. I never deserved you. I'm so sorry*. I make the dumbest promise I could. I promise Rachelle that I wouldn't harm myself. I don't know why. All I want is to be with her again. I just stare at her for what feels like hours, remembering all the perfect times we had together. I remember us

talking about getting married and how it needed to wait until I could afford a ring. I don't have money, and can't afford a ring, so I wanted to wait until I could get something worthy of her. She told me it didn't matter. I could make her a ring and she would still say yes. Before I leave, I take a ring I made out of my pocket and place it on her left ring finger. Now it's official. We're engaged.

I wait for everyone to have their moment with Rachelle, and then take my place waiting for her at the door. I want to see her again, just one more time, but I already had my chance. Rachelle comes to us pallbearers and we slowly and carefully place her into the hearse. I get into my car and take my place directly behind Rachelle's family. I light a cigar and take a deep breath. I'm shaking again. Things are becoming all too real. When we get to the church, I take my place at the head of the casket and slowly we bring Rachelle into the church. Her song is playing. It should have been our wedding song and instead it's the last song we'll ever hear together. The rest of her funeral is very religious. It should be. We are in a church. Rachelle is getting a full catholic funeral, which is very important. I take my place at my Rachelle's side and lead her out of the church. I put Rachelle into the hearse one final time and help her uncle close the door.

We get to the crematorium and Rachelle's mom makes sure we all stand in the room and push the button to turn on the machine. It's big and it's loud and I don't want my Rachelle to go in there. We count down and push the button at one. The giant furnace starts up and gets louder. As soon as the button is pressed, I pull my hand away. *You took her life. Now you take her body*. It's a whole different level of real now. I go into the observation room and it's full. So is the hallway and the entrance. People are even standing outside. I can't make eye contact without crying out loud, so I just stare at my hands. So many people came to say a final goodbye to Rachelle. You were so loved in life and not just by me.

We all go back to Rachelle's place for a celebration of life. The music is loud, the food is good, and the drinks are pouring. This is the kind of party Rachelle would have loved. I find myself looking for Rachelle to pull her close to me. I forget she's gone. My heart breaks all over again and I start to cry. I excuse myself from the party and sit outside of Rachelle's room. I dare not go into it. I cry and think about all the wonderful times I had and then guilt takes over. *You could have saved her.* I wipe my eyes and slowly make my way back to the party. A microphone gets passed around and anyone who wants to say something can. The mic comes to me and I say a little piece I wrote and read the first draft of the vows I was going to say to Rachelle. They aren't good, but they are just the first draft. I was going to add a bunch more stories and memories, but 'til death do us part came too fast. I pass the mic off and others say things, wonderful things, about my Rachelle. Everyone has a lot of stories and memories to share and I don't have many. Rachelle and I were both poor and couldn't afford big trips, or elaborate dates. We didn't want to. We just wanted to hold each other. *She deserved better.* Eventually the night turns into a sing-along. Rachelle's friends who can play instruments take over the mic and we all sing along to the songs they are playing. I can't stay anymore. I'm out of cigars and I keep looking for Rachelle. I miss my bed. I miss sleep. I pack my things and head to my car. I try to leave as discreetly as possible. As I say my goodbyes, everyone asks if I am okay to be home. I won't be alone. My parents are home and I'm on suicide watch, so my doors will be open.

I have a long drive home. I've been with Rachelle's family about 10 days while we got funeral preparations done. I forgot how much I hate this drive. Everything is going to be different now. *I feel worse than before. How is that possible*? I was on my deathbed even with Rachelle in my life. Now she's gone and I am worse. So much worse.

Chapter 7: Below the Bottom

I lay in bed and don't move. I don't sleep. I don't rest. I force myself out of bed once a day to check in with my parents. I put on a normal face, *whatever that means*, and speak with my mom and dad for a few minutes so they don't worry too much. Everything I do is dull, boring. All the things I used to do to relax just make me feel guilty. *I don't deserve to relax when Rachelle's gone*. I spend most of my time lying down, staring at my ceiling. I can't play video games. I can't watch the news. My social media is filled with Rachelle's face and I can't bear to see her right now. Food makes me feel sick. Everything makes me feel sick. I force a meal into my stomach, so my mom doesn't worry. She's always worried now.

I call my psychiatrist and set another appointment. He makes an appointment right away and tells me to bring everything I want. I bring my disability papers and he signs them within 10 minutes. I can't believe it. I have no words. My family doctor told me it would take hours. I fight back tears. He's making my life so much easier with just the flick of a pen. Why couldn't my family doctor do that? *He hates me*. On the way home from my appointment, I call my family doctor and tell him that after three times of not being taken seriously and almost killing myself, I will no longer be seeing him for my medical concerns. After 31 years, I'm done. I feel lighter. I am putting my health in the hands of someone who cares. I can't believe my family doctor. Why wouldn't he just listen to me?

Everything seems impossible. Eating, sleeping, breathing. I cry almost all day, everyday. When I'm not crying, I'm staring into space. My parents try to get me out of the house, but I don't leave my room. My friends try to get me to come out, but their invitations fall on deaf ears. All I want is Rachelle. Thinking about Rachelle is death by 1000 cuts. I can't stop thinking about her, but every time I do, a new wound opens.

After eight days of being home, I finally fall asleep. I see Rachelle in her room writing. She's writing her last notes. I try to reach out to her but my hand hits the thick glass I'm stuck behind. I knock on the glass, but Rachelle doesn't look up. I'm forced to watch as she puts the rope around her neck. I scream out Rachelle's name as tears stream down my face, but she can't hear me. Or she doesn't want to. As she drifts off to sleep, she looks up at my and reaches out just before her hand falls limp. I shoot awake in a cold sweat and check the time. It's 3:30 am. Our time. I run to the bathroom just in time to throw up. If that's my sleep, I'll just stay awake.

My doors must stay open. I get my privacy, but I can feel people checking in on me when I pretend to sleep. I don't really sleep. When I do, my nightmares make my sleep short and I'm tired of throwing up. I spend most of my night either watching the news or staring at my couch pretending to sleep. It's not just my family that has me on suicide watch. Rachelle's family checks in on me constantly and I have to respond. If I don't, my parents get a call. I feel like a lab rat, being watched constantly and responding on command like I'm being trained.

I reach out to my law friend. I need some good news. I hear nothing. I reach out to some other friends and hear nothing. I am falling apart, and you can't even say hello? *You're no friend of mine.* I spent my good years taking care of all my friends and now that I am the one who is in need, my 'friends' can't be bothered? I am done with so many people. I start saying goodbye to people who couldn't be bothered to offer support when I lost Rachelle. If you can't offer condolences, you don't deserve me in your life. I say goodbye to one person whom I haven't heard from in months. It might be online, but it does feel good to cut people from my life. Twenty minutes later there's a knock at my door and my mom yells up, "David, the door is for you, you're not in trouble". I'm terrified. If it was something good, why would she say I'm not in trouble? I don't want to go downstairs now. I go to the front door and see two police officers at the door. My heart sinks to my feet. They tell me that it's a safety call. Apparently, the person I told off called the police because I was acting out of character and it sounded to my 'friend' that I was going to self harm. I told the officers about my depression but that I was safe. Once they leave, I message the person telling them to never call the police on me again. If she didn't care to check in as a friend, she can't pretend to care now.

It's Rachelle's sister's birthday. She's going to a pub to celebrate and sends me an invitation. I don't want to be there. I don't want to be in public, but I want to make sure she's going to be okay, so I go. I miss Rachelle so much. I wouldn't know anyone there if it wasn't for her. I'm in a large group of friends and I feel so alone. I order a drink and pretend to listen to conversations people are having. Everyone is smiling and having a good time and can celebrate and be strong for Rachelle and her sister, and I can't bring myself to smile. Her sister can laugh and enjoy herself. She lost her older sister. Someone she's known her whole life, and I only knew her for a few years. Her strength gives me a moment of pause until a song on the radio plays. A song Rachelle and I would have danced to and she's not here. It's too much. I head outside and have a cigar. I never smoked before I lost Rachelle, so smoking is the one thing that doesn't remind me of her. I have a terrible time. I'm the designated driver because I can't drink on my meds. I smoke to escape the large groups of people in the bar having fun. Before the end of the night, my pack of cigars is gone, so I don't have an excuse to leave the group anymore. I'm stuck. I finally get to take Rachelle's sister home and sleep for about an hour before someone wakes me up by throwing up everywhere. I was mid nightmare anyways, so I just lay on the couch until morning and leave before breakfast. I just want to be home alone.

I go to a tattoo shop with an idea for a new tattoo. I've taken the song Rachelle wrote about me, converted it to a visual file and put an angel on either side. I'm so proud of the design. It looks beautiful and is the perfect tattoo for Rachelle. I originally wanted to put it on my arm, but they convince me to put in on my chest instead. It's designed to be close to the heart. It's perfect because that's where Rachelle still is. The angels have purple semi colons in their wings to represent mental health. The tattoo hurts more than I expect when the needles go into my sternum, but it's for Rachelle. The pain is worth it. With a little extra time, I decide to get another tattoo on my left arm of the last thing Rachelle ever wrote me: You are love.

Chapter 8: New Purpose

Some of Rachelle's friends create an event in Rachelle's honour. I offer to help in any way they need. Anything to do with Rachelle. I want to help as much as I can. I want to make sure it's worthy of who she was. I get to MC the whole night. We start off with a few words from me and the creators. I have a hard time speaking about Rachelle, but it's important, so I choke back tears. People sing and dance and everyone is having a great time. That's my cue to leave the party and have a cigar. I can't be around people having fun. It reminds me of having fun with Rachelle and I don't deserve to have fun without her. The hall is almost at capacity. There are so many people that I've never seen before. So many friends of friends. People who have heard about Rachelle and wanted to show her love and support. By the end of the night, I announce that we raised more than $5000 for the Centre for Addiction and Mental Health. Most importantly, we are donating the money in Rachelle's name.

Everything I do in Rachelle's name makes me feel a little better. I don't want to do anything for myself anymore. Everything is for her. We were on the same path in life. Doing things for Rachelle gives me strength. I post online about my mental health struggles. The people who tell me not to, quickly find their way out of my life. The more I come out in support of mental health, the more I can tell Rachelle's story. I meet new people who also struggle with mental illness. Being able to share Rachelle's story helps them with their struggles. She's still helping people from above.

I spend Christmas with Rachelle's family. I don't like Christmas and I'd rather be somewhere where it's okay to be quiet and miserable. It works. Christmas is quiet and I am miserable. I spend most of the time playing video games and crying with Rachelle's sister. Rachelle's presence is really missed, especially by me. Everyone has a shoulder to cry on, except me. I don't know where to turn, so I go up to spend some time in Rachelle's room and I just weep in my hands.

Our one-year anniversary rolls around. Today was the day I was going to propose. I was going to take her to a butterfly conservatory because she loved butterflies. I was going to take her on a wine tour because she loved her wine, and out for a steak dinner. I would have driven back to my apartment where we first met. I would have gotten on one knee in the snow and said 'Rachelle, from the day I met you, I fell in love with you. When you told me you loved me, I felt something I've never felt before. Safe. You are all I think about, all I dream about and I want today to be the first day of the rest of our lives. Rachelle will you marry me?' I would have slid the ring that I made onto her finger and she would have cried, and I would have cried. She would have said yes and then would help me up and we would kiss our first kiss as a forever couple. Today was supposed to be perfect. Instead, I can't move. Paralyzed with grief. Today was supposed to be the best day of my life and instead I'm reliving my worst.

Slowly, I'm starting to feel a little bit better. I can sleep without getting nightmares. I'm not crying everyday. I can visit with my family and am starting to enjoy the things I used to love. I can play video games. I can watch the news. I've even joined a soccer team again. Everyday is a struggle, but I am trying hard to build a new routine. I still wake up at 3:30am every day, but that has just become part of my routine. My psychiatrist is proud of my progress. He tells me I am doing more than most in my position. I'm still smoking too much weed and tobacco, but he tells me to go easy on myself. He says I'm doing so well that I don't need to see him for another three months. I feel proud that I don't need to see him every few weeks. Three months is a long time. He gives me enough refills of my medication to last me until our next visit.

Rachelle is still always on my mind. I miss her so much. My good days are worse than my bad days because I miss her more on my good days. When I am happy, I still look for her. Still want her by me. There's a piece of me missing. I still keep to myself most days, but I am doing better on my own. I can spend more time with my family and out with my friends. I always have tobacco on me just in case I start to panic. I'm starting to look forward. I have a plan for a mental health shoot, so I ask a friend to photograph me and I edit the photos myself. I like them. I share some of them online and get a great response. I get a few people wanting to shoot with me, which is wonderful. Photography used to be a huge passion of mine, so having it back in my life gives me strength. Rachelle gives me strength.

I find peace in art of any kind. When I'm not taking photos, I'm writing poetry or painting. I'm terrible at both, but it helps and that's what matters. I write a poem about how I am feeling since losing Rachelle. I photoshop wings onto a photo of Rachelle and project it onto a board. I take some paints, trace out the photo and paint it in. She looks beautiful. A friend of Rachelle's asks me for help training her dog. I haven't worked with dogs in years, but I used to be so happy working with dogs, so I accept. Working with her dog keeps me in the moment. I'm not worried or sad. I'm focused on the task at hand. It's better than I remember. For an hour, I almost forget about everything. Losing Rachelle, my anxiety, my depression. Everything. For an hour, I feel free.

Money is very tight. I'm spending more than I'm getting, and the bank froze my accounts because I'm behind on payments. I'm looking into bankruptcy because of my stupid roommates and my law friend has left me high and dry. *There's no one that can save you.* In a desperate attempt to get myself out of trouble, I reach out to my friends asking for help. I ask for $500 to unfreeze my accounts and raise $2500. Every donation brings tears to my eyes. I see the names of friends I haven't heard from in years. I have so many friends from my past reaching out to help. I look at the tattoo on my arm: you are love. I really feel like it right now.

If you look hard enough, you can see me smile from time to time. I'm smoking less tobacco and don't have to leave a room because people are having fun. I have a new routine that involves being outside and getting active. I can't do too many things in one day, but I can prioritize things in my schedule. I am not in good shape, but I am doing better. Better is good. I wake up at 3:30 almost every day and the nightmares are still bad, but I am able to fall back to sleep most nights. Rachelle's name doesn't just bring sorrow, pain, and guilt. It also brings courage and drive. I haven't felt driven since I lost Rachelle. I want to make myself better, I need to make myself better, so I can share Rachelle's story. When I do, it gives me the strength to see tomorrow, even if I don't want to.

I start to free write in a journal. It helps me organize my thoughts. I reminisce about my past and how things used to be different. I wasn't always a hollow shell of a man. I used to know what happiness was. I used to know what I wanted with life. Now I have to redefine what happiness is so I can feel it again.

I want to help others. Helping others brings purpose to my life. I've been through hell twice and have come out the other side both times. If I can share my experiences and how I got through them, I will. I want to reach as many people as I can. *How?* I want to do talks at schools. I think being able to reach people at that age will help. That's when Rachelle really started to feel her Depression. I want to write a book. I've never written anything before, but that doesn't matter. *Just start writing*!

Rachelle has given me direction and purpose. She came into my life when I was nothing. She showed me what love is and that I deserved it. She taught me how to be happy and to follow my heart, no matter where it leads. Most importantly, she taught me the value of life. She taught me all the things she couldn't learn herself. Rachelle had her own strong demons. She saw a doctor, took her medication, saw a therapist, was a very active advocate for mental illness, and surrounded herself with the people who loved her most. No matter what she tried, it wasn't enough. We were all too late. I can't let that happen to anyone else. If I can reach one person, just help one person off the ledge, my life has meaning again. For the first time in a long time, I have a plan. I don't know how to get where I want to go, but I know how to start, and so I write.

Manufactured by Amazon.ca
Bolton, ON

17652574R00028